14.00

HUNTERS GLEN ELEMENTARY SCHOOL
13222 Corona St.
Thornton, CO 80241

MW00955503

DATE DUE

JAN 27 2014			
			PRINTED IN U.S.A.

Countries of the World

Cuba

by William P. Mara

Consultant:
Juan Carlos Espinosa
Cuban Studies Coordinator
University of Miami–School of International Studies

Bridgestone Books
an imprint of Capstone Press
Mankato, Minnesota

Bridgestone Books are published by Capstone Press
818 North Willow Street, Mankato, Minnesota 56001
http://www.capstone-press.com

Library of Congress Cataloging-in-Publication Data
Mara, W. P.
   Cuba/by William P. Mara.
   p. cm.—(Countries of the world)
   Includes bibliographical references and index.
   Summary: Discusses the history, landscape, people, animals, food,
sports, and culture of Cuba.
   ISBN 0-7368-0068-9
   1. Cuba—Juvenile literature. [1. Cuba.] I. Title. II. Series: Countries
of the world (Mankato, Minn.)
F1785.5.M37   1999
972.91—dc21

                                                            98-13075
                                                                 CIP
                                                                  AC

Editorial Credits

Martha E. Hillman, editor; James Franklin, cover designer and illustrator;
   Sheri Gosewisch, photo researcher

Photo Credits

Joan Saks Berman, 20
Maresa Pryor, 10, 14
Photo Researchers/J. A. Hancock, 16
Picture Cube/Frank Staub, cover, 8
StockHaus Limited, 5 (top)
Unicorn Stock Photos/A. Ramey I, 18
William P. Mara, 5 (bottom), 6, 12

Table of Contents

Fast Facts 4
Maps 4
Flag 5
Currency 5

The Land of Cuba 7
Life at Home 9
Going to School 11
Cuban Food 13
Cities in Cuba 15
Animals in Cuba 17
Sports and Games 19
Holidays in Cuba 21

Hands on: Play Pepper 22
Learn to Speak Spanish 23
Words to Know 23
Read More 24
Useful Addresses and Internet Sites 24
Index 24

Fast Facts

Name: Republic of Cuba

Capital: Havana

Population: About 11 million

Language: Spanish

Religion: Mainly Roman Catholicism

Size: 42,804 square miles
(110,862 square kilometers)
*Cuba is almost as large as the
U.S. state of Pennsylvania.*

Crops: Sugarcane, tobacco, rice

Maps

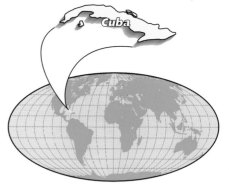

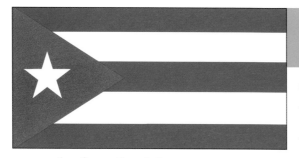

Cuba's flag has three blue stripes and two white stripes. Blue stands for the blue ocean around Cuba. White stands for the pure ideas of past Cuban leaders. A red triangle is on the left side of the flag. Red stands for the blood of people who fought for Cuba. A white star is in the center of the triangle. The star stands for the unity of Cuba's people.

Currency

The unit of currency in Cuba is the peso. One hundred centavos make up one peso.

In the late 1990s, about twenty pesos equaled one U.S. dollar. About fifteen pesos equaled one Canadian dollar.

The Land of Cuba

Cuba is a large island in the Caribbean Sea. Several small islands that surround Cuba belong to the country. Cuba is about 90 miles (145 kilometers) from the United States. Cuba is the same distance from Mexico.

Rolling plains cover much of Cuba. The Sierra Maestra (see-AIR-uh my-AY-struh) mountain range is in the southeast. Many beaches lie along Cuba's coastline. Forests of rosewood, mahogany, and cedar trees grow throughout Cuba.

Cuba's weather is warm all year. A rainy season lasts from May to October. Cuba has a dry season from November to April.

Cuba's warm weather makes it a good place for farming. Farmers grow sugarcane and tobacco there. Other common crops include coffee, rice, and bananas.

Rolling plains cover much of Cuba.

Life at Home

Most Cubans live in cities. Many Cubans find jobs there. About 20 percent of Cuba's population lives in Havana.

Many Cubans in cities live in apartments. The Cuban government owns many apartment buildings. Cubans pay the government to live in these places.

Some Cubans live in suburbs. These towns are near the edges of cities. Cubans who live in suburbs often live in houses.

Other Cubans live in rural areas away from cities and towns. Many of these people live in small villages. Some villagers use tree branches and leaves to build their homes.

Some Cubans live in rural areas.

Going to School

Children in Cuba start school at age five. They study math, reading, and history. Most Cuban students must wear uniforms to school.

Cuban students must attend grade school for six years. Many students go to middle school for three years. Some middle schools are boarding schools. Students live at these schools during the week. They go home on weekends.

Some Cuban students attend high school after middle school. They prepare for college there. Other students learn job skills at trade schools. The Cuban government also has many education programs for adults.

Most Cuban students must wear uniforms to school.

Cuban Food

Cuban food combines flavors from many areas of the world. People from Africa, Spain, and China have lived in Cuba. They created dishes from their native foods. Many of these dishes are now common in Cuba.

Rice and black beans are the main foods in Cuba. Cubans eat rice at every meal. Black bean soup is a common dish. Congri (kon-GREE) is a dish of rice and beans.

Cubans eat arroz con pollo (ah-ROAS KOHN POH-yoh). This common dish is rice with chicken.

Many fruits and vegetables grow in Cuba. Some people grow fruit in their yards. One popular fruit dish is fried plantains (plan-TANES). Plantains look like bananas. People eat pineapples and mangoes. Yucca (YU-kuh) is a common vegetable.

Rice and black beans are the main foods in Cuba.

Cities in Cuba

Havana is Cuba's capital and largest city. It stands on Cuba's northwestern shore. More than 2 million Cubans live in Havana.

One part of Havana is Habana Vieja (ha-BAH-nuh vee-AY-hah). This means Old Havana. This section of Havana has many historical buildings.

El Capitolio is in another area of Havana. This old Cuban capitol looks like the U.S. Capitol in Washington, D.C.

Cuba's second-largest city is Santiago de Cuba (san-tee-AH-goh DAY KOO-bah). This city lies in a valley in southeastern Cuba. About 500,000 people live in Santiago de Cuba. Many people work in the city's factories and shipping ports.

El Capitolio is in Havana.

Animals in Cuba

Several animals are native to Cuba. The Cuban crocodile lives in southern Cuba. This animal once was common in Cuba. Few Cuban crocodiles live in the country now.

Another native animal is the Cuban solenodon. Cubans call this animal the almiquí (ahl-mee-KEE). Cuban solenodons look like large rats. They eat insects. Very few Cuban solenodons are living today.

More than 300 kinds of birds make their homes in Cuba. Flamingos, Cuban parakeets, and buzzards are some of these birds. Other birds migrate to Cuba during winter. Migrate means to move from one place to another.

One of the smallest frogs in the world lives in Cuba. The microfrog grows to only one-half inch (about one centimeter). It is black with orange stripes.

Cuban solenodons look like large rats.

Sports and Games

Baseball is a popular sport in Cuba. Cubans enjoy playing and watching baseball. Cuba won first place in baseball in the 1996 Olympic Games. The Olympic Games are sports contests among athletes from many nations.

Many Cubans watch or play jai alai (HYE LYE). Jai alai players throw balls to one another with curved baskets. Soccer, basketball, and swimming are other popular sports in Cuba.

Board games also are popular in Cuba. Many Cubans play chess. Chess is a board game for two people. Players try to capture one another's pieces. Cuban Jose Raul Capablanca was the world chess champion from 1921 to 1927.

Baseball is a popular sport in Cuba.

Holidays in Cuba

Cubans celebrate several national holidays. They honor these days with parties and other events.

Cuban Independence Day is May 20. Cuba became an independent country in 1902.

Rebellion Day is July 26. This day honors soldiers who died in a 1953 battle. Fidel Castro led the soldiers. They were trying to change Cuba's government. Castro is now the president of Cuba.

Liberation Day is January 1. Castro came into power on this day in 1959.

Cubans celebrate these holidays in many ways. Schools and businesses close for the holidays. Cubans dance in the streets. They eat lechón (lay-CHON). Lechón is roasted pork. People drink refrescos (ray-FRES-kohs). Refrescos are cool drinks.

Cubans celebrate holidays in many ways.

Hands on: Play Pepper

Baseball is a popular game in Cuba. You can improve your catching and bunting skills by playing pepper. In this game, a bunter hits baseballs lightly with a bat to catchers.

What You Need

Four players
Three baseball gloves
A large playing area

One baseball
One baseball bat

What You Do

1. Decide who will bunt first. The bunter should hold the bat. The other players should wear the gloves. They are the catchers. The catchers should stand in a row about six feet (about two meters) away from the bunter.
2. Decide which catcher will throw first. That person throws an underhand toss to the bunter. The bunter bunts the ball. The ball should not go far. The catchers try to catch the ball. The catcher who catches the ball tosses it again.
3. Switch bunters after 20 pitches. Let each player have a turn at bunting.

Learn to Speak Spanish

boy	niño	(NEEN-yoh)
food	comida	(koh-MEE-dah)
girl	niña	(NEEN-yah)
good-bye	adiós	(ah-dee-OHS)
good morning	buenos días	(BWAY-nohs DEE-ahs)
hello	hola	(OH-lah)
house	casa	(KAH-sah)
thank you	gracias	(GRAH-see-ahs)

Words to Know

jai alai (HYE LYE)—a game where players throw balls to one another with curved baskets
migrate (MYE-grate)—to move from one place to another
rural (RUR-uhl)—away from cities and towns
suburb (SUHB-urb)—a town near the edge of a city
trade school (TRADE SKOOL)—a place to learn job skills

Read More

Crouch, Clifford W. *Cuba.* Philadelphia: Chelsea House, 1997.

Sheehan, Sean. *Cuba.* Cultures of the World. New York: Marshall Cavendish, 1995.

Useful Addresses and Internet Sites

Cuban Interests Section
Swiss Embassy
2630 16th Street NW
Washington, DC 20009

Embassy of Cuba
388 Main Street
Ottawa, ON K1S 1E3
Canada

Cuba Megalinks
http://www.laker.net/nike/megalinks.html
Excite Travel: Cuba
http://www.city.net/countries/cuba

Index

baseball, 19
boarding schools, 11
Caribbean Sea, 7
celebrate, 21
congri, 13
Cuban Independence Day, 21
Cuban solenodon, 17
Havana, 9, 15

microfrog, 17
Olympic Games, 19
plantains, 13
rural, 9
Santiago de Cuba, 15
Sierra Maestra, 7
suburbs, 9
trade schools, 11